OF DEMOCRACY
AMERICAN INSTITUTIONS

THE
U.S. MINT

THE HISTORY OF U.S. MONEY

EVERETT VOX

PowerKiDS
press.

New York

Published in 2018 by The Rosen Publishing Group, Inc.
29 East 21st Street, New York, NY 10010

First Edition

Editor: Elizabeth Krajnik
Book Design: Reann Nye

Photo Credits: Cover STILLFX/Shutterstock.com; p. 5 (both) NinaM/Shutterstock.com; p. 6 Roman Babakin/Shutterstock.com; p. 7 Historical/Corbis Historical/ Getty Images; p. 9 https://commons.wikimedia.org/wiki/File:NNC-US-1793-1C-Flowing_Hair_Cent_(chain).jpg; p. 10 https://commons.wikimedia.org/ wiki/File:Carson_City_Mint_(1866).jpg; p. 11 Courtesy of the Library of Congress; p. 12 Sergey Ryzhov/Shutterstock.com; p. 13 https://commons.wikimedia. org/wiki/File:NNC-US-1849-G$20-Liberty_Head_(Twenty_D.).jpg; p. 14 Kean Collection/Archive Photos/Getty Images; p. 15 Bloomberg/Getty Images; p. 17 https://commons.wikimedia.org/wiki/File:NickelReverses.jpg; p. 18 Alex Wong/Getty Images News/Getty Images; p. 19 https://commons.wikimedia. org/wiki/File:Boring-medal.jpg; p. 20 (Bicentennial quarter) https://en.wikipedia. org/wiki/File:1976_Bicentennial_Quarter_Rev.png; p. 20 (Bicentennial half-dollar) https://en.wikipedia.org/wiki/File:1976-S_50C_Clad_Deep_Cameo_(rev).jpg; p. 20 (Bicentennial dollar) https://en.wikipedia.org/wiki/File:1976S_Type1_Eisen-hower_Reverse.jpg; p. 21 Tom Grundy/Shutterstock.com; p. 22 https://commons. wikimedia.org/wiki/File:US_coin_25c_2015_ATB_Kisatchie_Unc.jpg.

Cataloging-in-Publication Data

Names: Vox, Everett.
Title: The U.S. Mint: The History of U.S. Money / Everett Vox.
Description: New York : PowerKids Press, 2018. | Series: Landmarks of democracy: American institutions | Includes index.
Identifiers: ISBN 9781508161011 (pbk.) | ISBN 9781508161035 (library bound) | ISBN 9781508161028 (6 pack)
Subjects: LCSH: United States Mint–Juvenile literature. | Coins–United States–Juvenile literature.
Classification: LCC HG457.V69 2018 | DDC 737.4973–dc23

Manufactured in the United States of America

CPSIA Compliance Information: Batch #BS17PK: For Further Information contact Rosen Publishing, New York, New York at 1-800-237-9932

CONTENTS

A NEW COUNTRY

The United States of America became a new country on July 4, 1776, when Congress approved the Declaration of Independence. This event would change the lives of everyone living in what were once the British colonies in North America.

Without Great Britain's control, Americans had to start over. They had to build their own government, write their own laws, establish a system of taxes, and create their own money.

The U.S. Constitution, which lays out the **structure** of the U.S. government, made certain issues very clear. When creating **institutions** in the new country, leaders had to make sure they weren't **threatening** the people's rights.

Today, the U.S. Mint falls under the control of the Department of the **Treasury**. The U.S. Mint makes coins, but it does not make paper money. The Bureau of Engraving and Printing, also under the Department of the Treasury, makes all U.S. paper money.

An image of the signing of the Declaration of Independence appears on back of the United States $2 bill. There aren't many $2 bills in **circulation**. Many people collect them.

MINTING THE MINT

Article I, Section 8, of the Constitution gives Congress the power to coin, or create, money. U.S. leaders needed to create a national **currency**, produce the physical coins and paper money, and **distribute** it to the people.

The Coinage Act, passed by Congress on April 2, 1792, created the United States Mint. After the Revolutionary War, people in the United States were using many different currencies from different countries. The Coinage Act created one **unique** currency for the new country.

CURRENT PHILADELPHIA MINT PHILADELPHIA, PENNSYLVANIA

The first Philadelphia Mint, or "Ye Olde Mint," was the first federal building built after the Constitution was **ratified**. In 1833, the government finished constructing a new mint building in Philadelphia to keep up with the demand, or strong need, for more coins.

The country's first mint building was built that year in Philadelphia, Pennsylvania, which was the nation's capital at the time. Making coins was a slow process because it required much physical labor.

THE MINT'S FIRST BATCH

During the mint's early years, it didn't produce many coins because there wasn't much demand. However, the mint used to produce a wider variety of coins than we have in circulation now.

The Philadelphia Mint's first batch of coins—11,178 copper pennies—went into circulation in 1793. After this, the mint started to produce coins using silver and gold as well.

American coins in circulation today are made up of several different metals. Pennies are made of zinc and very little copper. None of America's "silver coins" today are actually made of silver.

This "chain cent" from the Philadelphia Mint's first batch was sold for $2.35 million at a sale in Orlando, Florida, on January 7, 2015.

📍**INSTITUTION INSIGHT**

Coins in early batches of pennies are known as "chain cents" because the design on the back features 15 chain links that represent the 15 states in the Union at that time.

MINTS AROUND THE COUNTRY

The Philadelphia Mint is not the only mint building in the United States. In order to keep up with demand, the U.S. government added other mint buildings over the years. Currently, there are mint buildings in Philadelphia, Pennsylvania; Denver, Colorado; San Francisco, California; West Point, New York; Fort Knox, Kentucky; and Washington, D.C.

Congress authorized the Carson City branch of the U.S. Mint on March 3, 1863. It was built to make coins from the Comstock Lode, a large silver deposit discovered in Nevada.

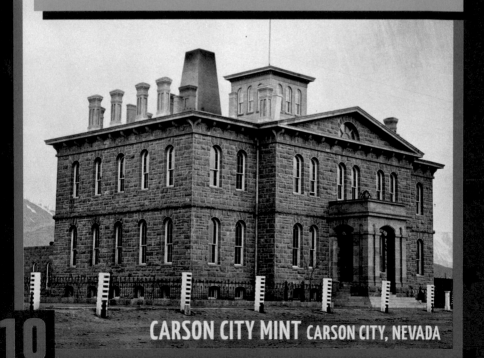

CARSON CITY MINT CARSON CITY, NEVADA

INSTITUTION INSIGHT

The second mint facility in San Francisco, known as the Granite Lady, was unharmed by the earthquake of 1906, which destroyed a large part of the city. The San Francisco Mint moved to a new building in 1937.

Each mint building has a different purpose. The mint's headquarters is in Washington, D.C. At the Philadelphia Mint, employees create plans for U.S. coins and medals and perform other tasks. The U.S. Mint stores bars of metal, called bullion, at Fort Knox.

11

WHERE DOES THE MONEY GO?

The coins that were made and circulated in 1793 are not still in circulation today. Where do these coins go after they are taken out of circulation? Old coins can be quite valuable, so some people collect them. As coins get older, many increase in worth.

INSTITUTION INSIGHT

Coin collectors are known as numismatists. Numismatics is the study of coins, paper money, and medals or the act of collecting them.

The U.S. Mint works as part of the U.S. Department of the Treasury to ensure that the country has enough currency in circulation. If coins are bent or worn down, banks can return them to the U.S. Mint, where they are melted down to make new coins. Coins stay in circulation for around 30 years, which is much longer than paper money usually does.

MAKING COINS

When coins were first made in the United States, the process required a lot of hard, physical labor. Horses powered the machinery used in the minting process. The modern minting process is much quicker and doesn't require hard labor, although the steps are the same as in 1793.

INSTITUTION INSIGHT

It took three years of working 11-hour days, six days a week, for coiners to produce the first 1 million coins at the Philadelphia Mint. Today, it takes about 30 minutes for workers at the Philadelphia Mint to produce 1 million coins.

Modern coining presses have made the minting process much quicker.

The six steps involved in coin making are: blanking (punching sheets of metal into coin shapes called blanks, today called planchets), annealing (heating the planchets to soften them), upsetting (raising the rim on both sides of the planchets), striking (stamping the planchets with the coin design), inspecting (looking over the coins to make sure they were made properly), and counting and bagging.

15

SPECIAL COINS

The U.S. Mint creates the coins that Americans use every day. However, the mint also creates special coins that aren't used as money. Some of these special coins are American Buffalo coins, American Eagle coins, and commemorative coins.

Commemorative coins are created to commemorate, or mark and honor, people and events from U.S. history. The U.S. Mint introduced the commemorative coin program in 1982. The sale of these coins helps raise money to build and maintain U.S. institutions and support different programs. These coins are only produced for a limited time. Since the program started, the U.S. Mint has raised over $500 million through it.

The backs of these nickels made from 2003 to 2006 commemorate the 200th anniversary of the Lewis and Clark expedition and the Louisiana Purchase.

STRIKING MEDALS

The U.S. Mint also creates medals that commemorate certain historic events and honor remarkable people. Some of these medals honor people who have made a difference in the United States or the entire world, including Rosa Parks and Pope John Paul II.

INSTITUTION INSIGHT

On June 10, 2014, the 65th Infantry Regiment, which was the last **segregated** military unit in the U.S. Army, was honored with a Congressional Gold Medal. This regiment served the United States from 1899 to 1956. Its soldiers, called the "Borinqueneers," were from Puerto Rico.

In 2012, people formed the Borinqueneers Congressional Gold Medal Alliance to help the Borinqueneers receive the recognition they deserved for their years of service.

The U.S. Mint strikes several kinds of medals. The mint produces Congressional Gold Medals, which are the highest nonmilitary awards in the United States. The U.S. Congress gives these awards. It also makes medals that are **replicas** of these gold medals. The secretary of the treasury gives the U.S. Mint permission to make national medals. These medals may be part of a series.

START A COLLECTION

Becoming a coin collector can be easy. The next time you see a U.S. quarter, flip it over. Do you see an eagle or do you see a special image? If you see a special image, that quarter belongs to the 50 State Quarters program. From 1999 to 2008, the U.S. Mint produced quarters that honored each of the 50 states.

BICENTENNIAL DOLLAR

BICENTENNIAL HALF-DOLLAR

BICENTENNIAL QUARTER

⦿ INSTITUTION INSIGHT

In 1976, the United States celebrated its bicentennial, or 200th anniversary. That year, the U.S. Mint produced 15 million three-coin sets. These coins included a quarter, half-dollar, and dollar. The U.S. Mint also produced copper nickel versions of each coin for the public to use as money.

The state quarters were produced in
the order in which the states ratified the U.S.
Constitution. The back of each coin has a
design that features things from that state.
Can you collect all 50?

LEARNING MORE

The U.S. Mint's history has been part of U.S. history for more than 225 years. During that time, the mint has built new facilities, updated the process used to make coins, and added special coin and medal programs.

The U.S. Mint's designers, sculptors, and engravers are some of the best in the world. In 2017, the United States was awarded two Coin of the Year awards at the World Money Fair in Berlin, Germany.

Touring the U.S. Mint's facilities in Philadelphia or Denver is a great way to learn more about the mint's history, what coins are in production, and the minting process.

BEST CIRCULATING COIN
2017 WORLD MONEY FAIR

GLOSSARY

circulation: The passage of something, such as currency, from place to place or person to person.

currency: The money that a country uses.

distribute: To share, sell, or otherwise spread something out.

institution: An established organization.

perpetuate: To cause something to last.

ratify: To formally approve.

replica: An exact copy.

righteousness: The quality of doing or being what is just or proper.

segregated: Separated from a main group based on race, sex, class, or culture.

structure: The manner in which something is built, arranged, or organized.

threaten: To show an intention to do harm or something unwanted.

treasury: A governmental department in charge of finances and the building in which the department does business.

unique: Special or different from anything else.

INDEX

WEBSITES

Due to the changing nature of Internet links, PowerKids Press has developed an online list of websites related to the subject of this book. This site is updated regularly. Please use this link to access the list: www.powerkidslinks.com/lod/mint